5.45

CW01080876

Sight Reading

VIOLA

A progressive method

Grades 3-5

Celia Cobb &
Naomi Yandell

Published by
Trinity College London Press Ltd
trinitycollege.com

Registered in England
Company no. 09726123

Cover design by RF Design, rfportfolio.com
Printed in England by Caligraving Ltd

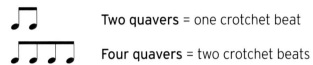

Lesson 1

- Practise reading quavers beamed in twos and fours
- Practise reading crotchet rests
- Revise the meaning of *Andante*

Quavers last for half a crotchet beat. They are often beamed in twos or fours:

Two quavers = one crotchet beat

Four quavers = two crotchet beats

Crotchet rest. A crotchet rest lasts for one crotchet beat of silence.

Andante means play at a walking pace.

Check the key signature. Then look at the time signature and note values. Notice any other details. Then play the whole exercise.

1
Andante

2
Moderato

3
Andante

4
Allegretto

5
Andante

Think before you play:

(This section applies to the duet below.)

	D major	G major
In which key is this duet?	☐	☐
At what tempo should you play this duet?	At a moderate tempo ☐	Quite fast ☐
For how many crotchet beats should you hold the longest note value?	Two	Three
What should you do in the rest in bar 4?	Stop your bow on the string	Retake your bow

Set the pulse. Look at the tempo marking and the time signature, and consider how fast you are happy to play the quavers. Then silently count a full bar before you lead in.

Only retake your bow when you are instructed to do so:

Otherwise, just stop your bow on the string during the rest:

Lesson 2

- Practise reading notes within the one-octave scale of C major, starting on the G string
- Practise reading minim rests

C major scale:

In C major you will use a low 2 (low 2nd finger) on the D and A strings.

minim rest. A minim rest lasts for two crotchet beats of silence.

Circle any notes that should be played with a low 2. Then look at the time signature and note values. Notice any other details. Then play the whole exercise.

Think before you play:

In which key is this duet?	C major	G major
What is the longest rest value in your part?	Minim	Semibreve
How many times should you use a low 2 on the D string?	Two	Three
Which bar contains the first five notes of C major scale?	Bar 2	Bar 7

 Duet

Your teacher will need to set the pulse for this duet. Listen carefully to the first bar so that you play at the correct tempo.

Notice the difference between semibreve and minim rests.

Semibreve rest. Lasts for four crotchet beats of silence, or a whole bar of silence in any time signature.

Minim rest. Lasts for two crotchet beats of silence.

Lesson 3

• **Practise reading notes in 1st position in the key of C major**

In the key of C major, the music will use notes from the scale of C major.

In the key of C major, you will use high 2s on the C and G strings, and low 2s on the D and A strings.

Circle any notes that should be played with a low 2. Then look at the time signature and note values. Notice any other details. Then play the whole exercise.

1

2

3

4

5

Think before you play:

From which scale should you take the notes?   C major ☐   G major ☐

Circle the low 2s.

In which bars is your rhythm the same as your teacher's?   Bars 4, 5, 7 & 8 ☐   Bars 2, 4, 5 & 7 ☐

Your bows will all last for minims in bars 4, 5 and 7.   True ☐   False ☐

 Duet   Set the pulse. Look at the tempo marking and the time signature, and consider how fast you are happy to play the quavers. Then silently count a full bar before you lead in.

 Before you play, speed read your part so that you are prepared for what is coming up.

Lesson 4

- Practise reading notes within the one-octave scale of F major

F major scale:

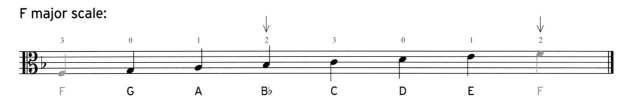

In F major you will use low 2s on the G and D strings.

Circle any notes that should be played with a low 2. Then look at the time signature and note values. Notice any other details. Then play the whole exercise.

1 Allegretto

2 Andante

3 Moderato

4 Andante

5 Allegretto

Think before you play:

In which key is this duet?	F major ☐	C major ☐
In how many bars should your **bow** play the rhythm-pattern ♩ ♩? (Think carefully!)	Two ☐	Three ☐
Which finger should you use to play the first note of bar 6?	High 2 ☐	Low 2 ☐
How many bars in your part have only one pitch?	Three ☐	Four ☐

Your teacher will need to set the pulse for this duet. Listen carefully to the first two crotchet beats so that you play at the correct tempo.

Before sight reading it is a good idea to play the scale of the key in which you will be playing.

Lesson 5

• **Practise reading notes in 1st position in the key of F major**

In the key of F major, the music will use notes from the scale of F major.

In the key of F major, you will use low 2s on the G, D and A strings, and a low 1 on the A string.

Circle any notes that should be played with a low 1 or a low 2. Then look at the time signature and note values. Notice any other details. Then play the whole exercise.

1
Moderato

2
Allegretto

3
Andante

4
Andante

5
Allegro

Think before you play:

In which key is this duet?	G major	F major
Which finger should you use to play the first note?	High 2	Low 2
You should play your part softly.	True	False
In which bars is your rhythm the same as your teacher's?	Bars 7 & 8	Bars 4, 7 & 8

  Set the pulse. Look at the tempo marking and the time signature, and look ahead to work out the tempo at which your bow will travel on the longest note values.
Then silently count a full bar before you lead in.

Moderato

 Looking ahead to think about bow speed will help you when you sight read. Long notes will usually need a slower bow speed.

Lesson 6

• **Practise reading notes within the one-octave scale of A minor**

C major and A minor share the same key signature:

A natural minor scale:

Circle any notes that should be played with a low 2. Then look at the time signature and note values. Notice any other details. Then play the whole exercise.

Think before you play:

In which key is this duet?	C major		A minor	
How many times should you play a low 2?	Once		Twice	
In which bar should you retake your bow?	Bar 3		Bar 4	
Every pair of quavers is played with one bow.	True		False	

 Duet

 Set the pulse. Look at the tempo marking and the time signature, and consider how fast you are happy to play the quavers. Then silently count a full bar before you lead in.

 The rhythm is probably the most important thing to get right when you are sight reading. But if you can read the key signature accurately, and spot details like slurs and dynamics too, then you are on your way to becoming an excellent sight reader.

Lesson 7

• **Practise reading notes in 1st position in the key of A minor, including accidentals**

C major and A minor share the same key signature, so the 1st position notes in A minor are the same as the 1st position notes in C major.

In Grade 3 these are the accidentals you need to know in A minor:

F♮   F♯

Circle any notes that should be played with a low 2. Then look at the time signature and note values. Notice any other details. Then play the whole exercise.

1

Moderato

2

Andante

3

Allegretto

4

Moderato

5

Allegretto

Think before you play:

In which key is this duet?   A minor ☐   C major ☐

Circle the notes you should play with a low 2.

You will need to use a low 2 in bar 3.   True ☐   False ☐

At what tempo should you play?   At a walking pace ☐   At a moderate tempo ☐

  Set the pulse. Look at the tempo marking and the time signature, and consider the speed at which your bow should travel. Then silently count a full bar before you lead in.

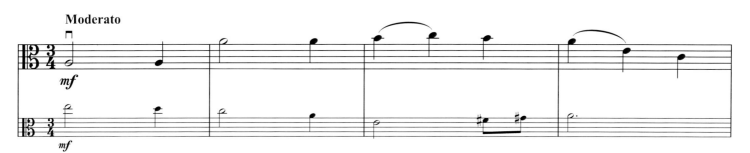

 Each accidental lasts until the next bar line unless it is cancelled by another accidental.
If an accidental is inside a bracket (♮), you still have to play it. It is just there as a helpful reminder.

Lesson 8

- Practise reading three-note slurs on one string, and two-note slurs across strings
- Revise the meaning of *mp*

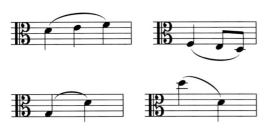

Play the slurred notes in one bow. Change note in the correct rhythm. The notes should sound *legato* (smooth).

Play the slurred notes in one bow. Change string in the correct rhythm. The notes should sound *legato* (smooth).

mp means play moderately softly.

Check the key signature. Then look at the time signature and note values. Notice any other details. Then play the whole exercise.

1

2

3

4

5

Think before you play:

From which scale should you take the notes?	C major ☐	F major ☐
Which bar contains five notes that move by step?	Bar 5 ☐	Bar 6 ☐
Circle the only bar in which you will need to use more than three bows.		
Should you retake your bow in this piece?	Yes ☐	No ☐

Duet

Set the pulse. Look at the tempo marking and the time signature, and consider how fast you are happy to play the quavers. Then silently count a full bar before you lead in.

Lesson 9

- **Practise reading notes within the one-octave scale of D minor**

F major and D minor share the same key signature:

D natural minor scale:

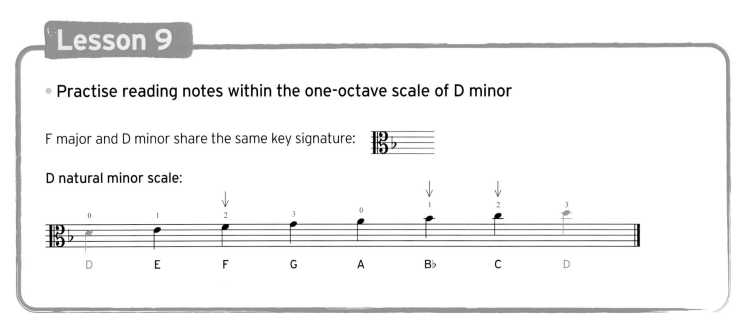

Circle any notes that should be played with a low 1 or a low 2. Then look at the time signature and note values. Notice any other details. Then play the whole exercise.

Think before you play:

In which key is this duet?

D major ☐   D minor ☐

The longest note values last for how many crotchet beats?

Three ☐   Four ☐

Circle the notes you should play with a low 1.

In how many bars should your **bow** play only crotchets?
(Think carefully!)

One ☐   Two ☐

 Set the pulse. Look at the tempo marking and the time signature, and consider how fast you are happy to play the quavers. Then silently count a full bar before you lead in.

Speed read before you sight read, and always look for patterns.

Lesson 10

• **Practise reading notes in 1st position in the key of D minor, including accidentals**

In Grade 3 these are the accidentals you need to know in D minor:

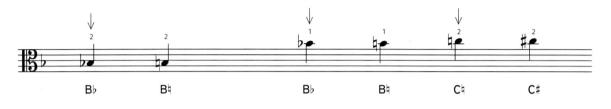

Circle any notes that should be played with a low 1 or low 2. Then look at the time signature and note values. Notice any other details. Then play the whole exercise.

1 Moderato

2 Andante

3 Allegretto

4 Moderato

5 Andante

Think before you play:

In which key is this duet?   D minor ☐   A minor ☐

Circle the low 1s.

Which finger should you use to play the C♯ in bar 8?   High 2 ☐   Low 2 ☐

Bars 5 and 6 have the same rhythm.   True ☐   False ☐

  Set the pulse. Look at the tempo marking and the time signature, and consider how fast you are happy to play the quavers. Then silently count a full bar before you lead in.

Before you sight read, always check the key signature and scan through to look for accidentals.
Remember, each accidental lasts until the next barline unless it is cancelled by another accidental.

Specimen sight reading tests

Remember to use the ideas and techniques from the previous lessons when approaching sight reading.

[Blank page to facilitate page turns]

Lesson 1

- Practise reading the dotted crotchet/quaver rhythm-pattern in simple time
- Practise reading quaver rests in simple time

♩. **Dotted crotchet.** A dotted crotchet lasts for one and a half crotchet beats.

A dotted crotchet is often followed by a single quaver ♪

Together they fill two crotchet beats: ♩. ♪ = ♩
    1 + 2 +   1 + 2 +

𝄾 **Quaver rest.** A quaver rest lasts for half a crotchet beat.

A quaver rest often appears with a single quaver ♪

Together they fill one crotchet beat: ♪ 𝄾 or 𝄾 ♪
    1 +   1 +

Check the key signature. Look at the time signature and note values, and any other details.
Then play the whole exercise.

1

2

3

4

5

Think before you play:

In which key is this duet?	F major ☐	D minor ☐
The best way to get the rhythm accurate is to:	Copy your teacher ☐	Count carefully ☐
Name the last note in bar 1.	F ☐	F sharp ☐
Every finger 1 is a low 1 in your part.	True ☐	False ☐

 Duet Set the pulse. Look at the tempo marking and the time signature, and consider how fast you are happy to play the quavers. Then silently count a full bar before you lead in.

 Counting '1+2+' etc. is called 'sub-dividing' the beat. It will help you to play rhythms accurately. Remember, unless you see a ⊓ or ⋁ sign in a piece of music, stop your bow gently during the rests and continue without retaking your bow.

Lesson 2

• Practise reading notes in 1st position in the key of D major

D major scale:

D E F# G A B C# D E F# G A B C# D

In the key of D major, the music will use notes from the scale of D major.

C# D E F# G A B C# D E F# G A B C# D E

In the key of D major, you will use high 3s on the C and G strings.
Watch out for C# on the C string, which you will need to play with a low 1.

Check the key signature. Look at the time signature, note values and other details.
Then play the whole exercise.

Think before you play:

In which key is this duet?	A major	D major
Bars 2 and 6 are identical.	True	False
Which bar contains only notes that move down by step?	Bar 3	Bar 7
In how many bars should your **bow** play the rhythm-pattern ♩ ♩.?	Two	Three

  Set the pulse. Look at the tempo marking and the time signature, and consider how fast you are happy to play the quavers. Then silently count a full bar before you lead in.

Remember to sub-divide to play rhythms accurately.

Lesson 3

● **Practise reading notes in 1st position in the key of B flat major**

B flat major scale:

Bb   C   D   Eb   F   G   A   Bb

In the key of B flat major, the music will use notes from the scale of B flat major.

C   D   Eb   F   G   A   Bb   C   D   Eb   F   G   A   Bb   C   D   Eb

In the key of B flat major, you will use low 2s on every string, and low 1s on the D and A strings.
You will also need a low 4 on the A string.

Check the key signature. Look at the time signature, note values and other details.
Then play the whole exercise.

Think before you play:

In which key is this duet?	D minor ☐	B flat major ☐
In which bar is your first low 4?	Bar 2 ☐	Bar 3 ☐
Which finger should you use to play the first note in bar 2?	1 ☐	Low 1 ☐
Which bars contain only low 2s?	Bars 1 & 5 ☐	Bars 3 & 4 ☐

  Your teacher will need to set the pulse for this duet. Listen carefully to the first four quavers so that you play at the correct tempo.

 Key signatures are important because they affect the positioning of your fingers on each string.

Lesson 4

• **Practise reading notes in 1st position in the key of E flat major**

E flat major scale:

In the key of E flat major, the music will use notes from the scale of E flat major.

In the key of E flat major, you will use low 2s on every string, and low 1s on the G, D and A strings. You will also need low 4s on the D and A strings.

Check the key signature. Look at the time signature, note values and other details.
Then play the whole exercise.

Think before you play:

In which key is this duet? Eb major ☐ Bb major ☐

Circle the bar in which you will need to play a one-octave arpeggio (going down).

In which bars do you need to play low 4s? Bars 2, 4, 6 & 7 ☐ Bars 2, 5, 7 & 8 ☐

You should retake your bow in the rest in bar 5. True ☐ False ☐

  Set the pulse. Look at the tempo marking and the time signature, and consider how fast you are happy to play the quavers. Then silently count a full bar before you lead in.

 Look ahead to spot any long notes, so that you can slow your bow as necessary. (Once it's gone, it's gone.)

Lesson 5

- Practise reading syncopated rhythm-patterns
- Revise the meaning of

Here are two common 'syncopated' rhythm-patterns:

1 2 (3) 4   1 + 2 +

Tap a pulse with your foot and clap some syncopated rhythms. Notice that they feel and sound a bit jazzy.

means **accent**. Play the beginning of the note with extra attack.

means *staccato*. Play the note with a short, brisk bow stroke.

Check the key signature. Look at the time signature, note values and other details.
Then play the whole exercise.

Think before you play:

From which scale should you take the notes?   B♭ major ☐   F major ☐

How many bars start with a syncopated rhythm-pattern?   Four ☐   Five ☐

Each syncopated rhythm-pattern is played on the same note.   True ☐   False ☐

Which finger should you use to play the last note in bar 6?   High 2 ☐   Low 2 ☐

 Duet   Set the pulse. Look at the tempo marking and the time signature, and consider how fast you are happy to play the quavers. Then silently count a full bar before you lead in.

 Notice the details, and include as many as you can when you sight read.

Articulation and dynamic markings show you exactly how to play the notes.

Lesson 6

● **Practise reading notes in 1st position in the key of E minor, including accidentals**

G major and E minor share the same key signature, so the 1st position notes in E minor are the same as the 1st position notes in G major.

These are the accidentals you need to know in E minor:

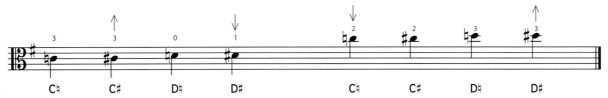

Sometimes there is a choice of fingering, for example you may choose to use low 4s instead of high 3s, or high 4s instead of low 1s.

Check the key signature. Look at the time signature, note values and other details.
Then play the whole exercise.

Think before you play:

From which scale should you take the notes?	D minor ☐	E minor ☐
Which bar is exactly the same as bar 1, but an octave higher?	Bar 3 ☐	Bar 5 ☐
The rest in bar 3 is worth four crotchet beats.	True ☐	False ☐
How many bars in your part do not contain a syncopated rhythm?	Two ☐	Four ☐

  Set the pulse. Look at the tempo marking and the time signature, and consider how fast you are happy to play the syncopated patterns. Then silently count a full bar before you lead in.

 The quicker you can spot patterns in the music, the easier you will find it to sight read well.

Lesson 7

• **Practise reading four-note slurs**

Play the slurred notes in one bow. The notes should sound legato (smooth).

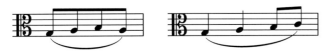

Check the key signature. Look at the time signature, note values and other details.
Then play the whole exercise.

1

Allegretto

2

Moderato

3

Andante

4

Andante

5

Allegretto

Think before you play:

In which key is this duet?	A minor ☐	C major ☐
In which bar do you repeat the quavers you play in bar 1 an octave higher?	Bar 3 ☐	Bar 4 ☐
Ignoring your teacher's part in bars 5 and 6 will help you to play the dotted rhythms accurately.	True ☐	False ☐
You should play the last two notes smoothly.	True ☐	False ☐

  Your teacher will need to set the pulse for this duet. Listen carefully to the first two quavers so that you play at the correct tempo.

 When you see a slur, remember that your bow will be moving more slowly than your left-hand fingers.

When you see:  your bow will play:

Lesson 8

• **Practise reading notes in 1st position in the key of G minor, including accidentals**

B flat major and G minor share the same key signature, so the 1st position notes in G minor are the same as the 1st position notes in B flat major.

These are the accidentals you need to know in G minor:

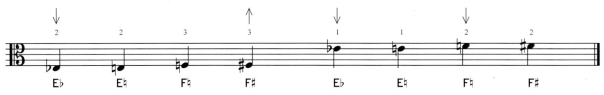

Check the key signature. Look at the time signature, note values and other details.
Then play the whole exercise.

Think before you play:

From which scale should you take the notes?   G minor ☐   D minor ☐

The key signature tells you that every A in your part is an A♭.   True ☐   False ☐

Circle the first high 3.

How many times will you need to play low 1 in this piece?   Once ☐   Twice ☐

  Your teacher will need to set the pulse for this duet. Listen carefully to the first three quavers so that you play at the correct tempo.

 Accidentals usually last until the next bar line. Sometimes composers may remind you to change back in the next bar (as in bar 4 of your teacher's part, above). Think for yourself as this is not always the case.

Lesson 9

- Practise changing between *pizzicato* and *arco*
- Revise the meaning of *crescendo* and *diminuendo*

String players often have to change between *pizzicato* (plucking) and *arco* (bowing). Speed reading before you sight read helps you to prepare.

Crescendo means getting gradually louder.

You may also see the word *cresc.* or the symbol:

Diminuendo means getting gradually softer.

You may also see the words *dim.* or *decresc.*, and the symbol:

Check the key signature. Look at the time signature, note values and other details.
Then play the whole exercise.

Think before you play:

In which key is this duet? C major ☐ A minor ☐

You should play only on the G string for the first four bars. True ☐ False ☐

In which bars should you get gradually louder? Bars 5-7 ☐ Bars 7-8 ☐

Circle the four-quaver tune pattern that repeats.

  Your teacher will need to set the pulse for this duet. Listen carefully to the first crotchet and quavers so that you play at the correct tempo.

 Check that you know how to change quickly and efficiently from *pizzicato* to *arco*, and from *arco* to *pizzicato*. Having a soft bow hold will really help.

Grade 4

Lesson 10

• Practise reading extra accidentals

Accidentals can sometimes occur outside the notes of the scale.

In this example, the key is D major, but there are notes which are not in the scale of D major: G♯ and F♮

Check the key signature. Look at the time signature, note values and other details.
Then play the whole exercise.

1

2

3

4

5

44

Think before you play:

In which key is this duet?   F major   B♭ major

Circle the notes that don't belong to the key.

Is every first finger a low 1?   Yes   No

You will use a high 2 to play the F in bar 3.   True   False

  Your teacher will need to set the pulse for this duet. Listen carefully to the first two quavers so that you play at the correct tempo.

 The details really count when you are sight reading. Always take a moment to speed read everything through before you play so that you can notice and incorporate as much as you can.

Specimen sight reading tests

Remember to use the ideas and techniques from the previous lessons when approaching sight reading.

[Blank page to facilitate page turns]

Lesson 1

- **Practise reading semiquavers in simple time**

♪ A **semiquaver** lasts for ¼ of a crotchet beat.

Four semiquavers last for one crotchet beat: ♬♬ = ♩

Two semiquavers last for one quaver: ♬ = ♪

Check the key signature. Look at the time signature, note values and other details.
Then play the whole exercise.

1

Andante

2

Allegretto

3

Moderato

4

Andante

5

Moderato

Think before you play:

In which key is this duet? B♭ major ✓   E♭ major ☐

Circle the bar with the syncopated rhythm in your part.

You will need to use a low 1 on the: D and A strings ✓   G, D and A strings ✗

The best way to get the rhythms accurate is to: Try not to listen to your teacher's part ☐   Subdivide the beat ✓

  Set the pulse. Look at the tempo marking and the time signature, and subdivide the beat to work out a good tempo. Then silently count a full bar before you lead in.

 Subdividing the beat will help you to play the rhythms accurately, eg in bar 4:

1 + 2 +

Practise reading bowing patterns

Two staccato notes played in one bow. Stop your bow crisply on the string then carry on bowing in the same direction.

Two tenuto (sustained) notes played in one bow. Stop your bow gently on the string then carry on bowing in the same direction.

Check the key signature. Look at the time signature, note values and other details. Then play the whole exercise.

Moderato

Andante

Moderato

Moderato

Allegretto

Think before you play:

In which key is this duet?

F major ✓   B♭ major ☐

You should stop your bow crisply on the string between beats 2 & 3 of bar 1.   True ☐   False ✓

Bars 5 and 6 are exactly the same.   True ☐   False ✓

In which bars should you play only low 2s?   Bars 2 & 8   Bars 2, 4 & 8 ✓

  Set the pulse. Look at the tempo marking and the time signature, and subdivide the beat to work out a good tempo. Then silently count a full bar before you lead in.

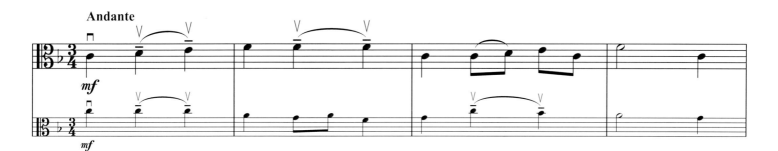

 Always speed read before you sight read. This will give you the chance to spot as many details as possible.

Lesson 3

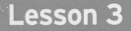

- Practise reading note values in the compound time signature $\frac{6}{8}$

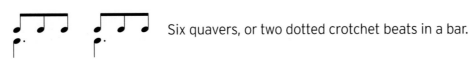

Six quavers, or two dotted crotchet beats in a bar.

These are some of the note groupings you can expect to see in $\frac{6}{8}$:

Check the key signature. Look at the time signature, note values and other details.
Then play the whole exercise.

1

2

3

4

5

Think before you play:

In which key is this duet?	G major ☐	D major ☐
Every finger 2 in this piece is a low 2.	True ☐	False ☐
How many bars in your part have only crotchets and quavers?	Three ☐	Five ☐
How long is the longest note value in your part?	Three crotchet beats ☐	Two dotted-crotchet beats ☐

  Set the pulse. Look at the tempo marking and the time signature, and subdivide the beat to work out a good tempo. Then silently count a full bar of quavers before you lead in.

In **6/8** when the tempo is slow, musicians tend to count in quavers.

But when the tempo is faster, they count two dotted crotchets in a bar:

Lesson 4

• Practise reading rests in the compound time signature $\frac{6}{8}$

Here are some of the rest/note groupings you can expect to see in $\frac{6}{8}$:

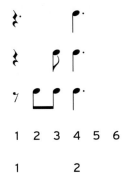

Remember, ▬ means a whole bar
of silence in any time signature.

Check the key signature. Look at the time signature, note values and other details.
Then play the whole exercise.

Think before you play:

In which key is this duet?	A minor	☐	C major	☐
The dynamic is the same throughout.	True	☐	False	☐
What should you do in the rests in bars 2 and 3?	Count & stay still	☐	Count as you prepare your up bow on the G string	☐
If you are counting in quavers, how many should you count for your last note?	Three	☐	Six	☐

Duet

Your teacher will need to set the pulse for this duet. Listen carefully to your teacher's part so that you play at the correct tempo.

In $\frac{6}{8}$ remember:

𝄾 or ♪ = one quaver beat

𝄽 or ♩ = two quaver beats

𝄽. or ♩. = three quaver beats

𝄼 or 𝅗𝅥. = six quaver beats

Lesson 5

• **Practise reading octave harmonics**

○ shows that you should play a harmonic. Lightly touch the relevant string half way along as you bow.

C   G   D   A

Check the key signature. Look at the time signature, note values and other details.
Then play the whole exercise.

1

2

3

4

5

Think before you play:

In which key is this duet?	F major	D minor
For how many quavers does the longest note last?	Four	Five
You should play the B flat in bar 7 with a low 2.	True	False
On which string should you play the harmonic in bar 5?	D	G

  Your teacher will need to set the pulse for this duet. Listen carefully to your teacher's part so that you play at the correct tempo.

Be aware: ° means play a harmonic.   0 means play an open string.

Think ahead: if you need to play a harmonic, prepare your left hand in advance wherever possible.

Harmonics sound best when you use a fast bow near the bridge.

Lesson 6

• Practise reading in the key of B minor

D major and B minor share the same key signature, so the 1st position notes in B minor are the same as the 1st position notes in D major.

These are the accidentals you need to know in B minor:

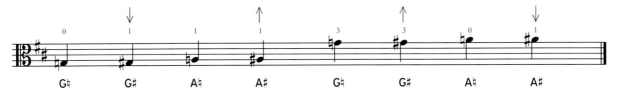

Sometimes there is a choice of fingering, for example you may choose to use a low 2 for the A♯ on the G string, or a low 4 for the G♯ on the D string.

Check the key signature. Look at the time signature, note values and other details.
Then play the whole exercise.

Think before you play:

In which key is this duet?	B minor	D major
How many bars in your part contain a syncopated rhythm-pattern?	One	Two
What should you do in the rest at the end of bar 4?	Stay still	Retake your bow
Which finger should you use to play the second quaver in bar 2?	3	High 3

 Duet Set the pulse. Look at the tempo marking and the time signature, and subdivide the beat to work out a good tempo. Then silently count a full bar before you lead in.

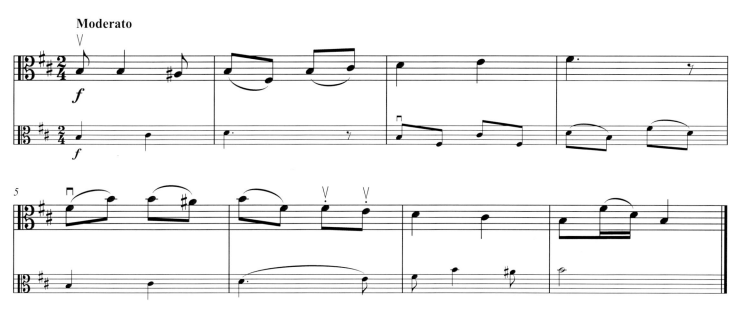

 Feel the pulse; this is especially important when you are playing syncopated rhythms.

Lesson 7

- Revise the meaning of *rall.* and *rit.*
- Revise the meaning of **tr**

rall. is short for *rallentando* and *rit.* is short for *ritardando*.
All of these words mean 'getting gradually slower'.

tr means play a trill. Your bow should last for the written note value.
Your left-hand fingers should alternate quickly between the written note and the note above.

Check the key signature. Look at the time signature, note values and other details.
Then play the whole exercise.

Think before you play:

In which key is this duet?	G major ☐	G minor ☐
What is the difference between bars 1 and 5?	The pitch ☐	The rhythm ☐
You will only need to use high 2s in this piece.	True	False
Which notes will you play in the trill?	B and C	C and D

  Your teacher will need to set the pulse for this duet. Listen carefully to your teacher's part so that you play at the correct tempo.

 Remember to take the key signature into account when playing a trill:

Use 1 and low 2:   Use 1 and high 2:

Lesson 8

- Practise reading in the key of A major

A major scale:

In the key of A major, the music will use notes from the scale of A major.

In the key of A major, you will use high 3s on the C, G and D strings. Sometimes there is a choice of fingering, for example you may choose to play G♯ as a high 4 on the C string, or as a low 1 on the G string.

Check the key signature. Look at the time signature, note values and other details.
Then play the whole exercise.

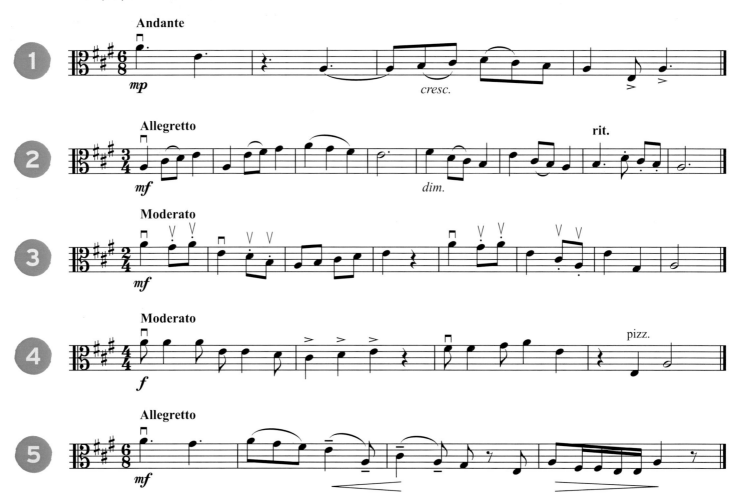

Think before you play:

In which key is this duet?	D major ☐	A major ☐
In which bars should you retake your bow?	Bars 4 & 5 ☐	Bars 4, 5 & 6 ☐
D is the only open string that you should play in this duet.	True ☐	False ☐
The first note in bar 3 is:	C ☐	C♯ ☐

  Your teacher will need to set the pulse for this duet. Listen carefully to your teacher's part so that you play at the correct tempo.

 In A major, the key signature tells you to play F♯, C♯ and G♯, so don't play the open C or G strings, unless they are marked as naturals.

Lesson 9

• **Practise reading in the key of C minor**

E♭ major and C minor share the same key signature, so the 1st position notes in C minor are the same as the 1st position notes in E♭ major.

These are the accidentals you need to know in C minor:

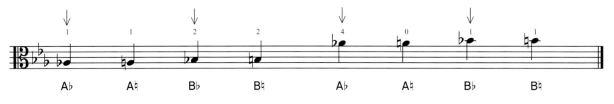

Check the key signature. Look at the time signature, note values and other details.
Then play the whole exercise.

Think before you play:

In which key is this duet?	E♭ major	C minor
How many dotted crotchet beats should you count in each bar?	Two	Six
Which finger should you use to play the first note of bar 2?	1	Low 1
You should play an open A string in bar 3.	True	False

  Your teacher will need to set the pulse for this duet. Listen carefully to your teacher's part so that you play at the correct tempo.

 Keep a steady pulse. In the duets in this book your teacher can see what you should be playing; in other pieces you may find that each player has a separate part so it's vital to learn to keep absolutely in time.

Lesson 10

• Practise reading extra accidentals

Remember that accidentals can sometimes occur outside the key.

As well as reading the key signature, you also need to watch out for extra accidentals. Accidentals often indicate a minor key, but they can be found in major-key pieces too.

This example is in E♭ major, but you will need to play some A naturals, which are not in the scale of E♭ major.

Check the key signature. Look at the time signature, note values and other details. Then play the whole exercise.

Think before you play:

In which key is this duet?	A minor ☐	C major ☐
Which notes in your part are not in the key?	F♯ and G♯ ☐	F♯ and B♮ ☐
The last quaver in bar 6 is a F.	True ☐	False ☐
What should happen to the tempo of the piece?	It should stay the same throughout. ☐	It should slow down in the last two bars. ☐

 Duet Your teacher will need to set the pulse for this duet. Listen carefully to your teacher's part so that you play at the correct tempo.

 These are the keys you can expect to find in Grade 5 sight reading:

Major keys – C, G, D, A, F, B♭ and E♭.

Minor keys – A, E, B, D, G and C.

Practising these scales and arpeggios regularly will help you to play confidently in these keys.

Specimen sight reading tests

Remember to use the ideas and techniques from the previous lessons when approaching sight reading.